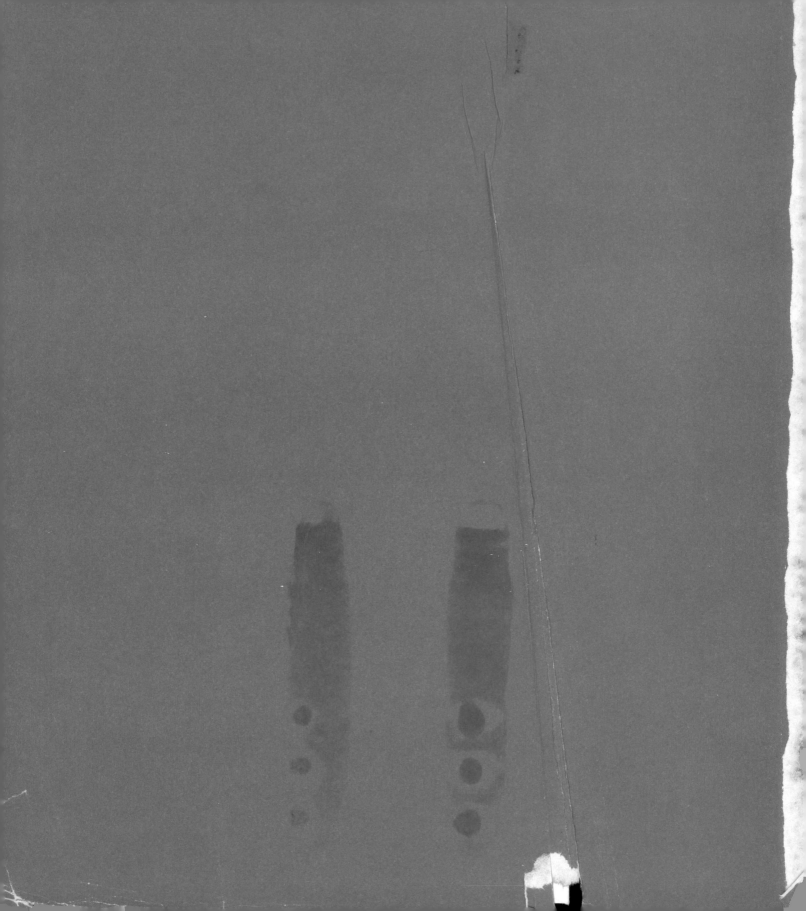

Old MacDonald Had A Farm

illustrated by

LORINDA BRYAN CAULEY

G. P. Putnam's Sons · New York

Illustrations copyright © 1989 by Lorinda Bryan Cauley.
All rights reserved. Published simultaneously in Canada.
Printed in Hong Kong by South China Printing Co.
Book design by Golda Laurens.
Music arranged by Susan Friedlander
Music typesetting by Music Book Associates, Inc.
Library of Congress Cataloging-in-Publication Data
Old MacDonald had a farm: words & music traditional/
illustrated by Lorinda Bryan Cauley   p.   cm.
Summary: The inhabitants of Old MacDonald's farm are described,
verse by verse.   1. Folk songs, English—United States.
[1. Folk songs, American.]   I. Cauley, Lorinda Bryan, ill.
PZ8.3.0434   1989   88-11562   784.4'05—dc19   CIP   AC
ISBN 0-399-21628-6
First impression

For my daughter, Sean Catlin Cauley,
with love
October 9, 1987

Old MacDonald had a farm, ee-igh, ee-igh oh!
And on this farm he had some roosters, ee-igh, ee-igh oh!
With a cock-a-doodle here, and a cock-a-doodle there,
Here a doodle, there a doodle, everywhere a cock-a-doodle; } *Refrain*
Old MacDonald had a farm, ee-igh, ee-igh oh!

Old MacDonald had a farm, ee-igh, ee-igh oh!
And on this farm he had some chicks, ee-igh, ee-igh oh!
With a chick, chick here, and a chick, chick there,
Here a chick, there a chick, everywhere a chick, chick; } *Refrain*

Repeat previous refrain

Old MacDonald had a farm, ee-igh, ee-igh oh!

Old MacDonald had a farm, ee-igh, ee-igh oh!
And on this farm he had some cows, ee-igh, ee-igh oh!
With a moo, moo here, and a moo, moo there,
Here a moo, there a moo, everywhere a moo, moo; } *Refrain*

Repeat previous refrains (2)

Old MacDonald had a farm, ee-igh, ee-igh oh!

Old MacDonald had a farm, ee-igh, ee-igh oh!

And on this farm he had some dogs, ee-igh, ee-igh oh!

With a bow-wow here, and a bow-wow there,

Here a bow, there a bow, everywhere a bow-wow; } *Refrain*

Repeat previous refrains (3)

Old MacDonald had a farm, ee-igh, ee-igh oh!

Old MacDonald had a farm, ee-igh, ee-igh oh!
And on this farm he had some pigs, ee-igh, ee-igh oh!
With an oink, oink here, and an oink, oink there,
Here an oink, there an oink, everywhere an oink, oink; } *Refrain*

Repeat previous refrains (4)

Old MacDonald had a farm, ee-igh, ee-igh oh!

Old MacDonald had a farm, ee-igh, ee-igh oh!
And on this farm he had some goats, ee-igh, ee-igh oh!
With a bleet-bleet here, and a bleet-bleet there,
Here a bleet, there a bleet, everywhere a bleet-bleet; } *Refrain*

Repeat previous refrains (5)

Old MacDonald had a farm, ee-igh, ee-igh oh!

Old MacDonald had a farm, ee-igh, ee-igh oh!
And on this farm he had some ducks, ee-igh, ee-igh oh!
With a quack, quack here, and a quack, quack there,
Here a quack, there a quack, everywhere a quack, quack; } *Refrain*

Repeat previous refrains (6)

Old MacDonald had a farm, ee-igh, ee-igh oh!

Old MacDonald had a farm, ee-igh, ee-igh oh!

And on this farm he had some rabbits, ee-igh, ee-igh oh!

With a sniff, sniff here, and a sniff, sniff there,

Here a sniff, there a sniff, everywhere a sniff, sniff; } *Refrain*

Repeat previous refrains (7)

Old MacDonald had a farm, ee-igh, ee-igh oh!

Old MacDonald had a farm, ee-igh, ee-igh oh!
And on this farm he had some horses, ee-igh, ee-igh oh!
With a neigh, neigh here, and a neigh, neigh there,
Here a neigh, there a neigh, everywhere a neigh, neigh; } *Refrain*

Repeat previous refrains (8)

Old MacDonald had a farm, ee-igh, ee-igh oh!

Old MacDonald had a farm, ee-igh, ee-igh oh!
And on this farm he had some geese, ee-igh, ee-igh oh!
With a honk-honk here, and a honk-honk there,
Here a honk, there a honk, everywhere a honk-honk; } *Refrain*

Repeat previous refrains (9)

Old MacDonald had a farm, ee-igh, ee-igh oh!

Old MacDonald had a farm, ee-igh, ee-igh oh!

And on this farm he had some turkeys, ee-igh, ee-igh oh!

With a gobble, gobble here, and a gobble, gobble there,

Here a gobble, there a gobble, everywhere a gobble, gobble; } *Refrain*

Repeat previous refrains (10)

Old MacDonald had a farm, ee-igh, ee-igh oh!

Old MacDonald had a farm, ee-igh, ee-igh oh!

And on this farm he had some lambs, ee-igh, ee-igh oh!

With a baa, baa here, and a baa, baa there,

Here a baa, there a baa, everywhere a baa, baa; } *Refrain*

Repeat previous refrains (11)

Old MacDonald had a farm, ee-igh, ee-igh oh!

Old MacDonald had a farm, ee-igh, ee-igh oh!

And on this farm he had some kittens, ee-igh, ee-igh oh!

With a meow, meow here, and a meow, meow there,

Here a meow, there a meow, everywhere a meow, meow; } *Refrain*

Repeat previous refrains (12)

Old MacDonald had a farm, ee-igh, ee-igh oh!

Old MacDonald Had A Farm